curse this blue raincoat

curse this blue raincoat

and other poems

Paul Robert Mullen

COYOTE CREEK BOOKS | SAN JOSÉ | CALIFORNIA

Copyright © 2017 by Paul Robert Mullen

All rights reserved. No part of this book may be used or reproduced by any means, graphic, electronic, or mechanical, including photocopying, recording, taping or by any information storage retrieval system without the written permission of the publisher except in the case of brief quotations embodied in critical articles and reviews.

Names, characters, places and incidents are documented fictitiously. Any resemblances to actual persons, living or dead, events, or locales are purely coincidental.

Printed in the United States of America

ISBN-13: 978-1-946647-04-7

25 24 23 22 21 20 19 18 17   1 2 3 4 5 6 7

Back cover photo © 2017 by Luke Rimmer
Author bio photo © 2017 by Andrew Kerr
Cover design © 2017 by Jan McCutcheon

Published by Coyote Creek Books
www.coyotecreekbooks.com

*for nobody in particular,
but with many in mind . . .*

contents

those curious words
the poet 3
spellbinding 5
façade 6
retribution 7
jack of all trades 8
status 9

inside looking out
saturday afternoon 13
last tuesday 14
contemplations 16
the old man two doors down 17
reality 18
sundown on the 68 20
to follow 22
and now 23
southport 25
carrier 26
death rattle 28
the fly 29
the aliens are coming 30
midnight 31
mercy 32
head in the clouds 34
hermit kingdom 36
la mujer de la tarde 37
graveyard shift 38
if i'm still among the living 40

long hot summer 41
everywhere 42
where she went 43
holy man 44
uprising 45
new life 46
city welcome 47
14:09 to paris – metz – luxembourg 48
victorian picture house 50

the afterglow
poem 55
changing of the guard 56
country music 57
the morning after 58
2016 59
the next phase 61
late night jazz 62

tribute
Roberta Flack 67
so long troubadour 68
Lonnie Donnegan 69
the day the star-man died 71

curse this blue raincoat
curse this blue raincoat 75

affairs
such a rare thing 83
déjà vu 85
trip 87

conversation over dinner	88
ex	90
the hunted	91
in montgomery terrace	93
the gallows	94
i danced with you	95
the gift	96
leave books out of it	97
5pm	99
college love	101
that day on the seafront	102
press play	103
reunion	104
triumph	105
ten-story heart-break	106
cappuccino town	107
truth hurts	110
woman or wine	112
i understand love less than i understand war	114
silver screen	116
the future	118
i'll never find the words	119
and spring is coming	121
waiting	122
is this desire?	124
lover	125

finale

impasse	129

foreword

curse this blue raincoat begins with a young man's epiphany at a poetry reading: that there is a person behind the words—*"a poet—what a thing to be!"* His curiosity is sparked. His heart is moved. His life is changed. And when we turn the page, then the next and the next, we evidence how the lifeblood of poetry has flowed from this significant moment.

There are other influences, namely Leonard Cohen, whose music is referenced in the book's title. The book is also peopled with he's and she's: ungodly holy men, munificent lovers, potential lovers both needy and independent, middle aged selves looking back to youth and forward to aging. People disappear: an old man, a girl with turquoise eyes. Through these personas, we witness desire, aging, youth, sex, relationships, middle age, manhood.

Paul's poems are also populated with voices. We hear voices of bravado and humility, voices of distrust, cynicism and praise.

Voices "embittered," voices pleading with us to "open up your arms," voices in pain, and those that offer "mercy."

By the time we are swimming into the halfway point, the ambitious title poem builds to a fevered pitch. The young man at the poetry reading in the book's beginning has now lived through many years and accumulated voluminous life experience that his heart pours onto the page. We are besieged with a voice of prayer, a voice that aches with desire for answers to questions that have no answers. The prayer that from the raw fabric of paradox makes art.

Some poems in *curse the blue raincoat* are a call to the authentic self. They also ask: "What is that authentic self?" The ongoing quest for authenticity clearly lies within the realm of poetry. For poetry is the place where everything belongs, the depository of the whole lot, "however insignificant" or majestic.

The old man passes the baton. The young man carries it as he transforms to the next old poet. *curse this blue raincoat* is a testament to this transformation. And through Paul's words, we experience a flourishing poetic mind, a writer "alive to chance."

Kate Evans
Author of *Call it Wonder*

"In my dreams I can see a love that could be"

—DAVID CROSBY, In My Dreams

one

those curious words

the poet

we shuffled into the theatre
in twos and threes
sitting on numbing, bendy plastic with
little leg room
for a tall guy like me

    chattering and murmuring
in anticipation of the poet
filling the spaces in the humid air
between the gathering
        and the empty stage

and then the poet ambled in

small, gaunt
liver-spotted; late 60's at a guess
with deep-set eyes behind tinted lenses –
renowned, distinguished
    but not particularly famous
though i admired him
without ever knowing him

he was a *poet – what a thing to be!*

he started to read
       under the acquiescent swell
of amber lamp-light
soft, vulnerable
wearing every line on his baggy sleeve –

a poem about his grandmother.

he began to cry
all these years later, and my defences
shattered
right there

helpless to his words
surrendered to his tears
as the theatre held its breath

those *curious* words

spellbinding

he spoke so beautifully
    that just one word
and the hearts
    of
a thousand women

would surrender

façade

does this make me a poet?
a voice?
    raising the dust
slicing flesh from
    the word
in the disquiet
      of grey winter

retribution

you were a better poet
than i was. i always knew it but i couldn't
ever admit it.
you were more articulate, too.
could hold a crowd. i could barely hold
a stare.
and don't you remember us both
stood there
in our sunday best?
aunties fussing
playing with our hair on
the church lawn?

the day you told me
i was dumb

the day you said i'd never be as
smart, as popular, as successful
as you?

at ten years old it hurt like hell –

that day on the church lawn
a numbness
        like novocaine

a
desire
like no other

jack of all trades

playing with the poem
is
a bit like golf.

you hack around a bit
surround yourself with the right people
fancy yourself as a
bit of a player;

the
only difference
with the poem is
you realise, as the sun descends on
the final hole
that everything you've
written
is
way
below par.

status

looking at that old man today
tired of life
and in the same room
a young boy
full of life

i thought
i must be somewhere in between
       looking out of the window
into
the empty garden

two

inside looking out

saturday afternoon

that smell of charred nicotine
    and i'm seven years old again;
my
grandad's living room
on a saturday afternoon

    sausage rolls and fruit cake in front of
the gas fire, cuddled up to ben
the black labrador
enchanted by the dancing transparent blue

mum and sister and nanna out shopping, braving
december rains
for the high street sales
    my fingers crossed for the full time scores
    pouring through
on grandstand
that comforting, monotone drawl

grandad snoozing

the timeless aroma of
stale pipes

last tuesday

the little girl
just started laughing,
ha ha ha
at her grandfather's funeral -
she really couldn't help it.

then her mother laughed too
though nervously so, and the laughter was contagious
since it spread down the whole row
until ten people laughed loudly
then twenty
thirty
madness in their eyes
and i couldn't stand it any more
so i left before they pushed him
into the furnace
and walked all the way across town
placed a bet on
the horses
an outsider in the 3:10pm
and a
banker in the 3:40pm

both felt pretty good.

i holed up in a titty bar
where i could free my mind
of that sickening laughter, then
three hours later, after darkness had fallen
alongside

a bottle
of the finest (and many
bikini bras and pantyhose)
i felt much better, and laughed
out loud,
    ha ha ha,
with scotch in hand
since both horses came in
with fine
odds.

i had my cash for the night
and i'd never have to bury
my father
again.

contemplations

i woke up
      this morning
and thought:

    my God,
        i'm older now
            than i've ever been
and
yesterday's child

will ever be

the old man two doors down

this old man
lived two doors down
and he wasn't just old
he was *really* old. still slugging it out
with the weeds on his front lawn as i left home
for work.

he was a nice old guy. read the papers for
the local sport - asked me how cricket was going
how i was bowling
if i was knocking the batsmen dead.

"remember son," he'd say
    "*all* batsmen
are stupid."

one frost bitten morning, mid-november i think
the old man
wasn't there anymore
roughing it with the weeds

i wondered why, but drove off
anyway.

i never did
    find out his name.

reality

it's a constant struggle
not knowing
    who or what you are
in a world
that demands to know

and each waking minute is a battle-
ground
when you don't know
    what you want, let alone
    what you need
in a world that demands to know

and it's a drain on the senses
trying to live up to expectation
potential
the longing
    of others.

job, car, marriage, children, mortgage
vacation on the costa del sol
summer house with
persian rug
and fake wooden floors
    in the latest shade of mahogany.

there are places i'd rather be
than twisting in this lament
    like a corkscrew wedged into
cheap wine

locked
in a world that leaves no stone
    unturned
no shadow
    in the shade
and no man
        young, old or indifferent

to do as he pleases.

sundown on the 68

there's needle in the night air
of manhattan tonight;
foreboding like
i've never known

and i see danger in the haste
of moving limbs
pounding through the shadows and the fading silver
the anxious
      main-street hustle

the early breaths of forming hurricanes
sweeping folk
into relentless scamper. into the
sharp sigh of twilight

and yet, amidst growing disarray
there's talk of laurel canyon
and the daughter divine;

the quake of text vibration
    what will we have for dinner, honey?
pasta?
pizza?
    something quick . . .

clogged exhausts
a screaming child, hungry for calm.

through the steam and the lurching

superstructures pressing
on the skyline
the subways full, the bars full
park benches draped in filthy rags
the madhouses *full*;
    the lost and lonely
pissing in the wind
regardless, shameless

they've seen it all before
they'll see it all again

eyes of the impoverished
fixed
on their own glory

fixed
on the thick soup blazing wilderness
of pier diem
banality

to follow

she didn't see it
or hear it coming
and the letter fell, helpless, in
the muddied gutter
postmarked
         cornwall.
an apology
to her mum, since she'd been
a real bitch
         over christmas.

mum meant well
as most do
but she did go *on* at times
unnecessarily.

the old man at the roadside
rushed to her aid, though his hip still ached
from over-work
and the driver screamed
in the dying
         light of another late september
dusk.

still, the postman
hurried along
sack on his back
         a mad, blind rush
to meet the
final collection.

and now

here we are
faulkner and i
counting our losses in
    the culvert of your excess.

you, racing towards fatality
through raging streets
consumerism
    apocalyptic optimism.

in the cities
arachnids wait patiently beside
resting heads, behind closed
    doors of stubborn oak
behind facades of contentment
jewels, temporary riches
    desperate mirth.

here we are
faulkner and i
one disguised in flesh
    and bone; such *trickery*
watching empires burn as the young
fuck one another
    irrespective
as they always did

    and the masses
gathered around their thorny crown
rebel

rebel
rebel

as they always did

here we are
faulkner and i
contemplating hell, as the skies grow cold
and the
    night owls scatter

southport

overlooking the dunes
you whisper to me
    that the rain must have killed her
as i start the
engine

carrier

    the fever
took a man down today in
the year of our Lord
        2014.

they were out with their blasters
      panic rising
roaring through the gutters
and the drains with
      bloodshot eyes

blasting!
blasting!
blasting!

when the smoke cleared
the stench was foul;
      lodged in people's
throats
like shards of broken glass
a stinging
strong enough
to put Kratos on one knee.

now, in the bowels of the
      marketplace, someone proselytising
spitting biblical thunder
screaming for the finale
nauseous with fear.
summer, rampant

immersed in its own husky, hazy steam.

the orange tree
    staggering
against the skyline; aged against the blossoming
youth of the new season.
        a blackbird
injured at the wing
delivering itself to the bushes
      to die.

        somewhere an echo.
        somewhere a miracle.

the day
    is taking shape.

death rattle

do you hear the screams of
the captive bird?

do you *hear*?

somewhere in the distance
    where the carnival roars
the glasses clink, and the
in-crowd
huddle
she is
dying.

our little force of nature
entombed
in a
wooden house

made for one

the fly

these loose chunks of soul
buzzing
    like never-ending
smoke detectors
around the delicate
        sound waves
of my brain

and though i recognise
that it is late
and that the smoky, ochre glow
    of my cool porch
provides
solace that a late-summer
riverbank cannot

i
curse
    whichever
higher power sent these
devils
into the dreamy, vanilla-scented
wasteland
of
my glorious
       cocoon

the aliens are coming

    in their droves.

no wonder
the leaves have withered
and
the babies
    left crying
for
something they can never explain
seem
    numb

in the enigmatic
shadow
of
tuesday afternoon's

    swan-song

midnight

looking out over the marina
stoned
out of our tree. she asks
if i see the shark?

she says it's beautiful,
 slicing
through the moonlit lake.

i tell her i think so, sit down.

the electric neon fuzz of the harbour
trying to focus on the people
the people   trying to focus
on the black   ocean   behind
   the promenade
watching
     the people
and the waves
focus   trying
on the people   on the waves

rolling
in
                        and out

mercy

standing over the fox tangled
in the wire
i see the compassion in your eyes
turn
to tears

though i just can't end it
    the man that i am
despite
dying sobs   fear in its eyes

do it, you say
do it

but i just
can't

a question of balance

it led me
    over rough terrain
until
we reached the gateway
    to infinity

where the mermaid lay
crowned
      intoxicated

head in the clouds

i graduated
as the new millennium was
in its infancy
and bounced around, chip on shoulder
expecting people to kneel
in admiration, bow before my
achievements, hold me
in high regard.

i sat cross-legged
back straighter than the
skyline
waiting for that knock on
the door. the golden ticket to
a dream job
    life of luxury
but then time ticked on
and before i knew it
there were more self-important
graduates bounding
about town. more delusion.
forever
expecting, ceaselessly presuming
and making
no plans
for themselves or their futures, just like
me.

now, years down the line, and
countless, brain abating, meaningless jobs later

i sit and wonder
where it all went wrong
and why there wasn't someone
to put their arm around my shoulders
and say
"hey, get off that cloud you're
living on, pal,"
so that i might have
realised; so that i could have discovered
that there wasn't anything special
about *me*
at all
so that i could have dropped
the pretence, the visions of
grandeur, the arrogance
expectancy
and the false dream.

instead i live embittered, hating the system
that failed me
and question, as i see kids
like me getting screwed
in the same way
every year
whether all hope
has gone, and whether
it was ever really there
to
begin with

hermit kingdom

imperialist
    or otherwise
the bogeyman of which you speak
is dead.

put down your banners
swallow your propaganda

cast away conjecture
and
    such deep mistrust

your wariness
is jaded.

at first light
    and at eventide

open up your arms.

la mujer de la tarde

at the fiesta   sweating
transfixed by the slaughter of the bull
visions of calvery. somewhere
the lunar cycle failing
agonies of self-contempt under
screams from
    the ferris wheel.

rotting fruit blurring vision
intoxication
engulfed by compli*cation*
hyperventilation
segregation

has the ferry left yet?

blinding sun under the volcano
bleeding into his eyeballs
apparitions of the sea
an illusory comfort.

   buenas noches!

turning to see her, fuzzy in the crowd
mind   failing
muscles
      numb

   buenas noches!

Paul Robert Mullen

graveyard shift

in he came.
she shuddered.
not this endurance test again.
he was convinced he had a chance.
she'd just turned nineteen.
he was thirty one. looked forty.
the bar was empty.
he noticed the lights had been changed.

"they're much better," he said.

she carried on arranging the glasses.

"i told her ages ago to change the lighting."

she felt awkward.
she didn't want to speak to him.
not after last week.

he couldn't remember last week.
he was still convinced
he had a chance.

"can i have a lager?"

she poured it without overspill.
he hated overspill. said it ruined the pint.

"a good pint always has a good head," he'd said.

that was before he said those other things.
she couldn't look him in the eye.
made her feel sick.
he pulled his phone out, pretended to text someone.
somebody came in, saw it was empty, shuffled out.
she hated this shift.

a newsflash on the big screen.

"son of a bitch," he said.

she didn't ask why. he *wanted* her to ask.
she started cleaning the coffee filter.
the music seemed a bit loud, he thought.
she wished the music was louder. the clock didn't seem to be
moving.
winter was closing in. a constant draft blew through
the side alley and into the bar.
passing headlights lit up the eastern wall where he sat.
the scar beneath his left eye
had never really healed. she turned away
when she heard engines approach.
the diary lay open beside russian vodka.
she wondered what shift she had
that weekend. the tv cut out again.

"*i* know someone who could fix that," he said.

if i'm still among the living

when the spring returns
in bloom
i'll walk this masquerade
alone
through the garrison
where you made me dance, polly-jean
in bleak pennine snows
years ago.

standing
    aged
with death and the lady
watching colours ripen once more
beside the
       black waterside.

i *will* remember.

long hot summer

she went missing that summer
    the girl with
the turquoise eyes. the hottest
summer for thirty years
the same summer that his lilies blossomed
    early

they thought she'd ran away
driven mad by
the full moon. they searched
and searched
but never found a trace

still his lilies grew strong
    a wonderful pale cream
and he cared for them sympathetically, slicing them
from their peppermint stalks with
precision, placing them in cold water
with a thumbnail of sugar.

for years
every sunday afternoon
    (if the weather was ok)
he'd take two or three to
blossom
where
she lay

everywhere

i hear your voice
everywhere i go

in the streets
in the sewers
in the squeals of the cinders of
the fiercest fires
inside the walls
in lavatories, factories
trains and buses
alleyways, asylums, and the cockpit
                flying south
the courthouses
the entrails of the theatre pit
inside the fizz of the champagne
bottle, and the minds of
the grand jury.

you are everywhere
to me

where she went

nobody knew

on the night train, alone

bounding free. chasing
down the
north-east winds
crying in the chapel
laughing
all the way to hell

abducted
        by the lone star
broken chains lying   naked
    in the passageways
of her mind

years ago we wondered

still
    i wonder

holy man

battered and bruised, i fought
my way through the
searing rain
into the depths
of the murky inn
where dishevelled old men chewed awkwardly on tobacco
and warmed their scaly gullets
with rum.

at the bar
a holy man, frayed and worn
and passionately drunk
with a gaze
so wild, tormented
he screamed, breathless
adamant that the word of God
was the only way to righteousness
virtue
sanctuary.

i moved to the bar, looked
at him closely. eyes sunken, corpse grey cheeks
teeth missing
matted silver hair thinning
tired bones cracking through
liver-spotted skin.

i ordered a whisky. made it a double.

the storm was upon us.

uprising

man's dawn awake

migration of the flock
in a dream
      celestial

new life

her promiscuity
    was nobody's concern

her addiction
    a recurring taboo

she lived on the docklands
to the east of the city

    bright lights

    blurred nights

an empty bed
        indefinitely

city welcome

holed up in a pokey backstreet
hostel, gare de l'est, paris. dim winter
lighting, a rotten
cheap wine head.

sat on the cold stone, third floor balcony
consumed by the grime and the gloom and
the smog. unsavoury, hooded
silhouettes wading
through the dog-shit, the litter and
the leaking drains. all around
romance dying.

being in paris won't make me a writer
just as putting on gloves
won't make me a fighter
clutching a rifle won't make me
a killer
or drinking all the wine in france
won't settle my thirst.

scratching my brain, i close the doors
pull across moth infested curtains
    where cockroach eggs, fresh in their gloop
    cling to rotting rails
close my eyes
and wait for
morning to arrive

14:09 to paris – metz – luxembourg

you've got to have balls to travel. you've got to
show grit and resolve, be fast-thinking, alert
take a gamble
chance your arm
follow your gut.

you've got to know how to stay calm
and collected. when to hide, duck and dive
latch onto the token
german with a map
and how to disappear
before they befriend you.

you've got to know how to catch eyes when
you need to appeal
to good nature. when to warn trouble
from your side. how to bounce back
when you take a swift right hand
when to run from the
shadows on continental
train platforms

who to trust

if you keep your wits about you
and your finger on
the trigger

you can really make it
alone
on the road

victorian picture house

we stood on the steps
    of the old victorian picture house
the one we campaigned to save all
summer long with our
banners and our flyers and our hearts and
our hopes

standing, watching the rush hour
    crawl by in the rich glare
of half-light. soon inside, hidden in the
shadows at the rear
the two of us once again, with that song playing
over and over
the one that gave me goose bumps
all summer long
summer of '96 –

and though we missed the film, exploring
one another's every breath
we walked out into the night
down the steps of the victorian picture house
young and content under a purple skyline
during those,

the days of our lives.

three

the afterglow

poem

open up your window, smell the
roses in the rain
taste the sea-salt in the breeze
watch the troubled getting wasted
on the beaches
at dawn
tigers dying in their cages
thunder
on the highways
a busker singing
spanish harlem

somewhere a string ensemble
somewhere a thief in the night

the seraphs crying in their sleep
and the lizard king
                      waiting

changing of the guard

the glorious summer
    has tumbled into
    november
and
the voices of the angels
are chanting
      deep within my thalamus
welcoming
the great poet
    home.

peering into an indistinct
future
i see only empty space
where
    the greats once stood.

the kettle is humming
    like a distressed bird
signalling time
for another caffeine injection
before
    the world
        carries on
            regardless

country music

country music
        she said

isn't complicated. it will either
make you laugh
or
break your heart.

just like waking up in
the morning
        i said.

the morning after

on the weekend that ballard died
my mind   disintegrating into camden lock
pretending to hear
        your testimony.

repelling affection   sexuality placed
carefully
        on the roulette board
the stench of clean metal
            a loaded gun.

serial killer
in the coffee house
reading the headlines.

2016

statues of the unknown
stand rotting in the snow.

winter will be over soon
and the passers-by, dwarfed beneath the wall
will come again. many years late
but here
all the same.

the fear of the rising
the hurrying of hooves
a darkening breeze.

small, clay town lying low under
a crescent moon
absorbing twilight
the failing winter
    and the screams of the
wolf.

sometimes i don't remember how we died
hearts thumping underground
gathering one another
in the dark

falling

danger
    like a fin emerging in a crowded ocean
weighing on the night

Paul Robert Mullen

and but for the absence of gods
the hummingbird
survives
      still singing
her song of hope.

this memory
forming out of silence
on the day of Cohen's death
marching
      through the idle forests
      of one's conjurings

just a timid love
left
    smiling at me

to keep me warm

the next phase

transition
re-position;
   red brick terrace
drenched at sunrise

   premonition
       realised

late night jazz

in the abso*lute*
sifting;
all-consuming, soul
capturing
    ivory tingle with sad
    sax, painting
the night blue

smoke cloud café
stale nicotine liberation
in the rush
of stillness

    late. gin soaked, oh
so late
feet eaten by
high-hat rattle, slide bass
frag
       menting reality, time,
reason.

no chance of escape
before sky
    detonates
    sunrise, or not
so long as
jazz robots, burning muscular
receptive wonder
beat-
stricken

invite
my mind's eye
to

paradise

four

tribute

Roberta Flack

it was as though
i was sat
overlooking a quiet river canyon
at dawn
    when i first heard her sing
that song

it was as though
    an angel divine
was there at my side
behind a tempest of splintered ivory
amidst the quietude of
a sleepy storm
deep and warm
roaring softly
    up against the tiny hairs, stood
    on end, at the
base of my
    neck

so long, troubadour
for Leonard Cohen

there is no light
shining
    through the cracks
in
anything
    today

only
    the feint murmur
of that
husky voice
    lodged
inside
my
    conscience

Lonnie Donnegan

was singing
with a rattle and a hum
something about a muleskinner
on the rock-island line

such enchanting tones
spiralling
through the rustic smoke
    of grandfather's pipe

my eyes drawn
to the hypnotic motion of the LP record

rising and falling
    rising and falling
        rising and falling

the needle like a vessel on a
stormy sea.

years later i'd shake his hand
old onnie
in the theatre lobby of a
sea-side town –
    him, almost done
    me, just beginning

the man who captured
lennon; a catalyst
for rock revolution

Paul Robert Mullen

with his hand in mine
for those brief moments
in 1999

me, just short of seventeen;
a zenith
in my days
of
luke-warm
    insignificance

the day the star-man died

sitting
invigilating an exam
in the stinging bite
    of chinese mid-winter

mind in some nomadic
quest
    for warmer shores

and then the vibration
working its way north from my trouser-leg
through my hip
my latissimus, ribs, and into my throat
where it lodged a little
before the signal
        struck my cortex

a flood of messages
since people already knew

a moment when you can barely understand
the meaning of it all
the *point* of it all

him, gone

the sound of horns
        bouncing on the airwaves
across the boundaries
of the universe

Paul Robert Mullen

five

curse this blue raincoat

curse this blue raincoat

i pray for a response to beauty
to the wonder in this landscape
in this being
in these objects;

i pray for a response to this curious emanation
we call *beauty*
this power in a vision
a touch
a breath of air on a mountain top
the colours in the sky and the scent
    in a wildflower
the pain in the face of the singer
whose passions have overwhelmed them
to the humbleness of genius
the cries of broken hearts in hell
the magnificence of new life, and the miracle
of sexual union

i pray for a response to the thunder in
the words of the poet
the bright lights when we close our eyes
the wrinkles on your skin in the dead of night
to those who rejoice as the fires ravage the horizon
those who turn their backs on hope
the winners and the losers
the frenzied thoughts of my youth and the
    words of the prophet

i pray for a response to love

Paul Robert Mullen

    and friendship
to the privileges we are afforded in dark times
to passivity
curiosity
obsession and religious kitsch
to recklessness and falling rocks on the horizon
the oceans and the blazing summer
    and the savage in an honest tongue
to the unacknowledged legislators of the world
the sensory overload of the piano
the joy lying hidden in the artist's brush
the reflection in a window pain
to the failure of enterprise and the commandment
    of success
to the labours that arise from *loving*

i pray for a response to
paradise
to apathy
victory upon victory
the sharp united rebels, the surrender to mediocrity
those who play the heroes in their own dramas
life after death
comic strips   superheroes
the hunt, and birds of prey
to footsteps on the dance-floor
to the preface of the translation
    and the monasteries hidden in jungles
    hidden in thought

i pray for a response to the raven and
the dove
the naivety of age

to big ideas in tiny minds
the end of a night at the start of a journey
evaporating popularity
    increasing popularity
(evaporating
again)
to superstition
communism
the notion of forever
the healing powers of zen
the protocol of sacrifice and the
    quest for martyrdom

to the *final* delivery

i pray for a response to the march
    the beating of the drum
    the ringing of the bells
and the silence of the solo rider –
to the zeppelin in flight, heading back to the end
    of the beginning
the backstreets of paris in summertime
to krishna, and the epic play
raised glasses for the call of duty
liars in dimly lit subways
the embrace
    of rival armies
to the tangled circumstances of existence and the
    signs on
the road to nowhere

i pray for a response to her irrational love for me
and mine

to the wisdom of the fool
the good old days and the inconceivable future
the stigmas that our eyes devise
    and the horns on the unicorn
to the sweeping echoes across
the moors, to the bruised fortunes of doomed sailors
    and the mystery of the israelites
to our mind-numbing colleagues
    that eat away our souls
and the blackbird in
the silver beech

i pray for a response to the final supper
to the man who suffers for his art
the sisters of mercy, and the falcon who sails
    on the crest of the tsunami that crushes the harbours
    of the world
to the turbulence in sharing
the weakness in the lion's eyes
the rituals of the orderly
    and the world's deepest thinkers who
carry such weight

identity
divinity
her silhouette in the moonlight
to the guru and the lessons learnt at dusk
the warriors still battling
    already dead
the pin drop and the snow flake
to the humility in murder, the dread in the mind
of the boxer
and the truth   impossible

      to locate

i pray for a response
      to temptation
to the evils in the bloodstream
the perils of knowledge
   1969
and the magnitude of infinity

to the lifeless rivers flowing
(blood red)
my own creations, however insignificant
the rabbit in the headlights
to the constellations on a hot august night
the religions of the world
and
    unbearable periods
of
   eruptive
       silence

six

affairs

such a rare thing

    now that i remember
the streaks
of silver-white light from
    a winter morning sun pouring through
the blind like
elderflower wine, striping your face
etched in sleep
peacefully
    content.

that is how i remember you

calm, motionless
the subtle rise and fall
of your chest in time
with the timid white breakers
    lapping the edge
of dry land

like
    the only survivor on
a paradise island the morning after
a great storm, you lie, dancing through your imaginings
waiting for the daylight
to unravel your dreams
    waiting
for that salty touch of my lips
upon your lips
to rouse you

Paul Robert Mullen

      from another plane

years later
    as i struggle to recall your voice
i can't help but wonder if
you remember me
   where you are
and if
those rays of light
that illuminated that beautiful scar beneath
your brow
all those years ago
      have left any
mark
   at all

déjà vu

it was that fine rain
on an opaque afternoon; the skies
as grey as grandmother's eyes
the night before
        she passed

the churning seas stalking the land
like a killer
        with their victim
in sight

the crunch of shingle awoke me
from my slumber. the racket
        of a fist against glass
her naked shoulders just
a memory
        a scatter
of lights
        in the shadows of the headlands
beaming across the bay

something inside me
stirred
like i'd been here before
    as the colours in the skies
changed, bleeding
into twilight
like the oil from an artist's brush
and the
        boom boom boom

Paul Robert Mullen

of that fist
      a jackhammer in my brain
crashed
against my temples

i was overcome
by an offensive love
      so disastrously beautiful
so far away

you see
    by nature
i'm so gentle

i beg you never
to forget

trip

little miss strange with her
china cup. her patchwork eyes looking deep into
mine. somewhere in the room the gods
making love
in the kaleidoscope
of the midnight lamp. the sound of
traffic standing still. walls swaying electric. starlings
     laying down heads on shoulders
of white night
        neon grooves.

marshmallow weariness;
no such time
no such thing.   no such thing
as time
is the house burning down

    (on this) rainy day number nine?

conversation over dinner

"…so, what do you *do*?" she asked.

"i do lots of things, and nothing
at all," i replied.

"what d'you mean?" she frowned.

"just what i say."

"you're difficult," she said.

"not really," i said.

"i can't ever get a straight answer
from you," she complained.

"ask a straight question then," i said.

"*describe* yourself to me," she said.

"how many words?"

"just do it," she said.

"i'm just a man; a nobody
a somebody, a lover of winter
a chauvinist, a mediocre poet, a failed
drunk, a tax dodger
conversation evader, inherent gambler
and i like to

intimidate other peoples' dogs."

stunned, she rolled
a cigarette. i assumed
it was time to go
drained my bottle
smiled politely, paid the bill
and left.

another one down
      i thought
strolling slowly along
the promenade
      towards the dawn

ex

she disappeared to county armargh
or derry
or belfast
    or morroco maybe

i don't remember.

sending me postcards
what she was doing
who she was with
how much she wished things had
worked out. then
one day
they stopped coming.

for six years i kept them
in a shoebox for safe keeping
at the back of the
airing cupboard, until one morning
    springtime i guess
i took them into the garden
and buried them next to old jake

fists clenched
    blood red

the hunted

now she has
what she always wanted;
me   in her bed
a cold, naked heart
in the
summertime.

bodies
entwined
sweating through august nights
the dawn breeze, soft
through
an open window.

ending, in her arms. drunk
climax
deafening
a hand rested softly
upon my chest.

and yet
i resent her pleasure
i resent her control;
me   the wild animal
    caged
tamed

i resent   this counterfeit love
i resent   being owned
i will   *never*

Paul Robert Mullen

be tamed.

walking into town through the busy
odorous crackle
of dusk

voices
laughing
my
voice
    cracking

and that was all i had

in montgomery terrace

was it only yesterday?
twenty-four hours
    since you kissed my heart
awake?

such
small love
on a blue-grey morning. the clock
ticking away
in tune with the cockerel
as dawn, eaten alive by
a roaring sun
        rumbles.

    shattered dreams ignited.

such small love
    at daybreak

the gallows

i see something
in
your eyes
    that even words
cannot
  define

and i know
as the
    poets of the world
squeeze
their brains dry
that
i must break you

gently

i danced with you

after dark
in the sodden fields

two minds
one love

wired

the gift

you look at me once
wipe your eyes
look again
    tell me that
silence is a gift at times
        like this

and i think
this is not silence, this roaring
clap and crack in my temples
this volcanic dread.

    walking away
after handing you the keys.

now that was silence
    like i'd never heard before.

leave books out of it

a hand on my shoulder.

without looking
it was *her*
delicate palms, cucumber lotion. wanting to
ask me about literature
so i suggested we get a drink
sit down, talk it out
her eyes
never leaving mine.

sensing a long one, i checked the wallet
since the last time i ended a debate
on the greats
i was eight pints deep
and ready to roll

i said miss havisham was tragic.
she said she was evil.
i said oscar wilde was genius.
she said he was conceited.
i called chinaski heroic.
she called him a misogynist.

then
she came at me
eyes uneven with vodka
trampling my opinions like cockroaches
in the alleyways of her
own self-righteousness

Paul Robert Mullen

this mundane, rehearsed bullshit
that men so often endure

all the while (as she delivered her
vitriol)
forgetting that
she wanted
         to fuck me.

taking her was easy.

smiling, because she thought
she'd won.
thought she'd put me
in my place; and i hated her
right there and then

the moment
i almost certainly
fell in love

5pm

city folk
young and old
spilling out of office blocks
like molten lava as the clocks
gave them back their
lives.

"meet me at the met-bar,"
she said,
"two blocks west."

i took the car
since the weather was a mess
waited in a lay-by
one street away.

it was definitely *him*.

ageing, ailing
still paying the bills
whilst his wife
      ran about town
without regret
or
shame.

he pulled away
wheels trundling
spitting shards of rain
into the thudding mist

of ash grey
rush-hour.

"shit," i murmured
before
pulling away
too

college love

i sat and watched the man
speak softly
about the after-life
underneath
the dull rattle of
    faulty air-con
spring of 2001
when all i knew of you
was that red streak
in your shock
of jet black hair.

he was a tall man;
and dead soon after

about the time that i was holding you
closer than
i ever thought i would
in some sort of
    sweat-stained
teenage
matrimony.

Paul Robert Mullen

that day on the seafront

i saw you today
walking along the harbour hand-in-hand
with another man

your secret life blown
wide open.

still, the waves tumbled in
the mountainside reflecting gold
seagulls singing
to the witches in the pinewoods
children laughing at the world
as minutes
turned into years.

i spotted that the lush
vanilla ice-cream looked good
cheap, too
dripping white, toffee shavings

the bench
        by the sand
with room
for one

press play

as sure as there is someone in the world
    sleeping
and someone in the world
      wide awake

they will never accept our love

those
painting my days
black
    with fear

reunion

putting her hand on mine
over the plate glass
coffee table

saying with a smile
"things that don't end badly
      never end."

then, kissing; her lips
honeyed
like cherries
in the summertime.

through the window, seeing her walk away
into city crowds.

the future behind me.
the past
laid out ahead
      once more

triumph

this immaculate union

such insignificant love
framed
    in these four walls
    our four walls
of rapture

just my skin
    your skin.

in this union
we will
    overcome

ten-story heart-break

you didn't have to
look back
but i thought you would
and so i waited
until the crowds engulfed you;
         chewed you up
in that final, dusty portrait
of heart-racing despair
    hoping beyond hope
but
realising then
       that i'd never see
those eyes again
those spectral, marmalade eyes
for so long hidden by sprinkles of leaves
    at your window, over-
grown

that meeting of eyes. the consummation
of what was
and
    what will never
be
    again

cappuccino town

she stank of expensive white teeth
starbucks coffee
         and prada
cross-legged
with just enough thigh
to
charge my loins

    tall
sleek, arguably beautiful
i stared *into* her
    waiting for a sign.

it was then i remembered the
cruel significance
of those oily
bath times; a sympathetic mother
tortured
by her son's ailments
the sting
        of cold water
biting at my ankles
knees, buttocks
lower back.

the resounding thought:
why would she be interested in me?
sucking on a joint
like a meaningless past conquest
squeezing the air

    like a reddened pustule
with her clenched fist.

recalling
the aquiline nose of grandmother
slaving over
        late sunday afternoon beef,
heavily seasoned
and crackling in its final stages
of partial cremation.

    grandmother assured me
that the Lord was by my side
during the persistent trials of
the hours,
days.

fresh latte
        sparkling hot
forming
suggestive white froth upon
her glistening upper lip
somehow sparking thoughts of earth's long, dark history.

maybe it was the way her eyes
narrowed
in the flickering midday reflections
of an auburn sun
or
the way her glittering nails
curled around the coffee cup like
the tentacles
        of a serpent

poised
to sink a ship.

such reveries.

sinatra, slick upon the soundwaves
coffee mocha. moist carrot cake. idle talk
        and rumour
spreading
like a parasite

a glance at the immaculate quiff
rosé iPhone 6
        migraine on the 68

and a pocket full of mumbles
in the ears
of a man
ready to
        shed his skin

truth hurts

she sits there
dapper in drapes and purple beret
talking like machine-gun fire
about how the world has let her down
     failed her

and i sit
cabbaged by her tone
riddled with terminal
disinterest
the walls caving in
all around me
my mind wondering how
    i ended up listening to all this gash
in the first place
why i'm forever ending up
ensnared
by these agonising, doom-laden
self-important
     fools.

"you're the one
who dropped
your knickers," i interject.

"and that's why your cards
were dealt."

she reeled.
i rallied.

"that," i continued, "is why your life is
a mess."

sat, silenced
tears flooding to her stranded eyes
she exhaled
      as i slowly finished
my cinnamon infused
ice-mocha
      whilst contemplating
changing
the subject

woman or wine

she called me up late
    very late
demanding that i see her.

"not now," i said.

"*now*," she said.

"it's late," i said.

"it's gonna *be* too late
if you don't, you fucking…."

i hung up
pulled myself out of my armchair.
took a piss. washed my face.
looked in the mirror.

the phone rang again.

i didn't answer.

the nights seemed peaceful when i
was alone.
no noise, no lies
no arguing
backbiting, fighting
no distractions, no struggle for air.
nothing.

i opened another bottle of cabernet shiraz
an australian 1998.

outside my window
the world rumbled
chaotically
towards dawn

i understand love less than i understand war

with war you know where you stand.
when it's time to wave the white flag. when it's time
to pull the trigger.
time to run. hide. mount a chase. drop the bomb.
    strike.
you know when you have won
and when you've gone and got
your ass whipped.

love is different. you never *quite* know where
you stand. one minute you are making out.
the next you are making plans
for divorce
blocking bank transfers, cutting off the phones
changing locks.

i'm tired of all the anger
the bitterness, the frustration and resentment.
the arguments, the bitching
the lunacy.
i'm tired of slashing car tyres, shitting through letterboxes
chopping up designer clothes
and punching the walls.

i'd rather listen to neil young
than fall in love.
i'd rather shoot some pool, read some ginsberg, hemingway.

go for a swim, eat a curry. count the stars
until my eyes sting. play my guitar 'till my fingers
bleed.
walk my dog in torrential rain.

i'd rather settle
for everyone else's dreams
than fall in love.

now even *that*
is
slightly less painful.

silver screen

as my finger-tip scans
the nakedness of your spine
in the deteriorating hours
       of our final days
riding the wave of
each vertebrae
until your shoulders tense with quiet satisfaction
   i realise
that utopia is not the glittering
prize at the end of the rainbow
or sundown in paradise
as the breakers caress tepid
white sands

but
it is simply
   the purity of my breath, your
   breath
the study of your apertures
in the lounge-room
    mirror

the foggy voice of gene lockhart
   smouldering
barely audible
the soundtrack
to our moment
that moment
   once,
and

forever once
for
    ever

the future

someday you will find me
in the rooftops of your mind, with the
starling
and the pale moon

sharing solitude with eternity
holding out
for your eyes
      again

i'll never find the words

i'll never find the words
for the smell of lavender after
a rainstorm

or
    the smoky bacon charcoal buzz
of a roasting joint
upon
simmering coals

and
i'll never find the words
to tell you
    how
the summer sun bleeds
the
toxins from my mind
my *skin*

how
sinatra
brings me to my knees;
such quiet devastation
in the wee
small
hours

and i'll never find the words
for
    the aftermath

Paul Robert Mullen

of impulsive sex
            at dawn
or
the twisted lock of hair
at the base
of the stairs
            signalling the departure
of
a former life.

the only words i have
are
      these

i truly hope
that is
         enough

and spring is coming

finding you motionless
under the willow tree, numb
from the trials of the hours
eyes so heavy
        streaks of
salt and pepper
littered
in your mane

the rare, warm sun of mid-winter
canvassing
        the foothills
of mount belzoni

an empty bottle
        a loaded pen

end-
        less
possibilities

waiting

no words
    of any poignance
have left my lips
today
let alone my pen.

   walking through
alleyways
    at night
peering through windows
as
   relationships crumble
in front of reality tv
is
not even enough
to
   inspire words.

not even the sad smiles of
beaten housewives
or the crunch
   of the traffic accident
nor
the rush of cold blood
from the gaping heart
   of the adulterer's spouse
is enough.
i'm going to put this pen
away
   in a closet

with the dust
and the spider's webs
and
    hope
that some day
i'll be inspired enough
        by something
to
    open the door
    and my mind
and
    the floodgates

is this desire?

tearing down the walls
of my resolution?

setting me alight
    in the dark
on the
foothills of a private
miracle?

    in the deepest depths of sleep
in the places i never knew
    existed?

blind
    to reason?

alive to
chance?

lover

come
put your head
on my shoulder
and look out upon the open ocean
one final
    time.

there are no words.

there is
    no need.

seven

finale

impasse

how can i
      possibly
tell you
that
    i still love you
but
only as
    a memory?

The following poems in this collection have been previously published in the following literary journals, poetry magazines and e-zines:

"the poet" – *The Cannon's Mouth* – Issue 28, June 2008

"last tuesday" – *The Interpreter's House* – Issue 39, October 2008

"to follow" – *Fire* – Summer 2008

"head in the clouds" – *Dreamcatcher* – Issue 22, Autumn 2008

"city welcome" – *The Cannon's Mouth* – Issue 28, June 2008

"victorian picture house" – *Decanto* – October 2009

"that day on the seafront" – *Borderlines* – Issue 44, Summer 2009

"truth hurts" – *The Journal* – Issue 22, Summer 2008

"i understand love less than i understand war" – *Iddie* – Issue 4, Spring 2009

Paul Robert Mullen was born in Southport, near Liverpool, England, in 1982. He is a writer, musician, and University Lecturer, currently living and working in Nanning, Guangxi, China. His poetry has been widely published in a variety of literary journals, magazines and e-zines. He is also an avid blogger.

www.mushythebeatle.wordpress.com

www.mushythebeatle.blogspot.be

fb.me/PaulRobertMullenWriter

author.paul.mullen@gmail.com

www.ingramcontent.com/pod-product-compliance
Lightning Source LLC
Chambersburg PA
CBHW070448050426
42451CB00015B/3393